I Love You
Baby Girl

A heartbreaking true story of child abuse and neglect

Desire Night
Melody J. Laughlin

Shadowfyre Publications
San Diego, California

I Love You Baby Girl

ISBN: 978-1482593716

Published by: Shadowfyre Publications

www.shadowfyre.net

Dedication

I would like to dedicate this book to all the people that reached out and helped me. For the families that took me in when no one else would. I would also like to make a dedication to three women that played an extremely vital role in my life at my darkest hour. Three women Brenda, Barbara, and Elaine, each gave of themselves, opened their doors, shared their families, and taught me what being a strong woman was about. These women freely gave of themselves because they believed in a girl who we shall refer to as Sarah.

To my husband Richard who has faithfully supported all of my endeavors throughout the years.

Table of Contents

Acknowledgements

I would like to acknowledge the families that helped me over my childhood years; without your support, I do not know if I would be here today to write. To the Reed's, Sweet's, Reasoner's, Larkin's, and Carvin's, I thank you!

Prologue

2004

She was barely able to make out the words on the other end of the phone. The woman's voice gurgled, strained; finally she pieced it together, "I love you baby girl." That sentence played in her head repeatedly before she finally drifted off to sleep, on the overnight flight from San Diego.

1972

"Did you break my jewelry box Sarah?" Alex demanded.

She heard her father screaming, and yet her mind was not registering what was happening. She was only five and was already too familiar with that tone. The tone that made you hide under your bed and wish that you were invisible until his anger would fade away. There not going to be any hiding opportunities this time for he had already grasped her arm. He was twisting it and yelling at her, his face menacingly close. She could smell the alcohol on his breath, and knew that she was going to be crying before this day was over.

She frantically glanced over at her mother who was just sitting there watching with a blank stare on her face. You see, the five year old had witnessed who dropped the jewelry box earlier in the day, her mother had. Surely, she thought, mommy will tell him the truth. Yet she did not dare plead for help, instead she looked at her mother with tears in her eyes, silently imploring.

Her father shook her abruptly and demanded an answer, "Did you break my jewelry box?"

She responded quickly "No, I did not touch it."

Her father glared at her. "Liar! Your mother said you did!" and he slapped her so hard across the face she fell down. "Go get the belt" he bellowed.

She knew better than to ignore his request, and so she scrambled to her feet and brought the thick leather belt to her father.

Gazing over to her mother, her eyes once again silently implored, "Please help me, tell him the truth, please." Once again, her mother gazed back at her with a blank stare; she was going to have to take the fall for something she did not do. At that moment, she felt she was truly all alone in the world.

That night, in his drunken stupor, he beat her repeatedly with the belt. Though she cried and cried, there was no one there to help her, or make the pain go away. The property owner that lived below them would not even try to help anymore. Unfortunately for Sarah, in 1972, there were no stringent child protective laws and people only did so much.

Later that night her father left to go to the bars, a nightly ritual. Her mother was watching TV, and she sat down next to her and asked,

"Mommy why did you tell him that I broke the jewelry box?"

Her mother looked down at her and said quietly "Because you did."

2004

While starting the descent into Albany, she awoke with a start. She wiped tears from her eyes, gazed out the window and whispered softly to herself, "She lied to him because she could not stand another beating herself. " As she took a deep breath, she tried to suppress the words "I love you baby girl" from echoing in her head.

CHAPTER ONE

Ruth

Growing up in poverty stricken upstate New York was no picnic. Ruth was Ethan and Mary's seventh child out of nine, and the second daughter. Because Ruth was a girl, Ethan showed Ruth favoritism. Even with eight other siblings, Ruth had her share of hard work, and being the second girl, she was required to help Mary with the younger children. That was a lot of responsibility for young girl growing up.

Ruth's father met the criteria for the typical Irishman stereotype; a hard-working man loved by all and had a great sense of humor. However, Ethan was also known to consume his wages at the bars. This left remarkably little for the family to survive on, and the basics like food and clothing were scarce.

Ruth grew up wanting to escape the world she was in, and she was willing to do anything for that escape. When she met Alex, a local gang member, she thought maybe all of her dreams had come true. Alex was a charming young man who also came from a large family, and was the youngest of 15 children. They were both 16 when they met and Ruth's father was adamantly against them getting married. He knew of the reputation that Alex and his older brothers had around town and he did not believe that Alex would be a good match for his youngest daughter Ruth.

The two young lovers would not be denied, and before long, they ran off together, travelling with a group of carnies and working the circuit. This was the first time that Ruth had anything to call her own. The money she made she could use to buy new clothes and Alex treated her like his queen, they lived on the fringe, but they were happy.

Their happiness only lasted a few months before Evan found his daughter, dragged her back home and had Alex arrested for taking a minor over the state line. As soon as Alex got out of jail the two ran off again, in what would become a vicious cycle. Alex and Ruth would run away, and Evan would find them and drag Ruth home. Though he never again had Alex arrested, he often thought about having him killed. However, those were just thoughts that Evan had, for though he hated Alex, he loved his daughter, and knew that if he hurt the boy, Ruth would never forgive him. Finally, Ruth reached 18, and there was nothing that would stop her from obtaining what she wanted, and that was to marry Alex. Evan finally agreed, and the wedding plans began.

The two were married in September of 1964, in a modest ceremony with close friends and family at the Stone Street Presbyterian Church. Alex was in between jobs and so the newly married couple ended up moving in with Ruth's parents. They were still living there 9 months later when Sarah was born.

Perhaps it was a case of post-partum depression, or maybe it was the fact that getting married did not solve her problems, but after

Ruth gave birth to Sarah, she experienced a mental breakdown. Back then, treatment of clinical depression resulted in a stay at the St. Lawrence Psychiatric Center and Ruth was no exception. Leaving her young infant Sarah in the care of her mother, Ruth was hospitalized for nearly 6 months. During this time, Alex moved out of the house, not wanting the responsibility of caring for a newborn on his shoulders. He went back to his gang and began traveling down the path of alcoholism. That was the only way he knew how to deal with the fact his beloved Ruth was in the "loony-bin."

During the time Ruth was hospitalized, the infant Sarah did not adapt well to life outside of the womb. She was a colicky baby and allergic to all types of infant formula. Back then lactose intolerance was not, well known, and babies were either breastfed, or fed milk-based formula. It was not like today, where there are all types of formulas to provide for individual needs. Sarah was exhibiting symptoms of Failure to Thrive Syndrome, and steadily lost weight until they found a diet, which she could tolerate. After being switched to fresh buttermilk and squash the constant screaming stopped, and her grandparents were given some much-needed peace.

Alex would come over to see the child from time to time, though he truly blamed the baby for her mothers' breakdown. Alex resented Sarah so much, that he began to hurt the child on his visits. One time Evan caught Alex touching the tip of a lit cigarette to the infants arm, burning her. Evan became enraged and literally threw Alex out of the house, telling him that he was no longer welcome. Alex did not come back until the day Ruth was released from the psychiatric center.

When Ruth was finally released from the hospital, she was ready to resume her life, but she immediately noticed that things had changed in her relationship with Alex. Alex seemed distant and cold to her, and he had immersed himself in his gang. He spent most of his time out drinking with the guys.

Alex came to pick her and the baby up the day she got home from the hospital, and took them to their new apartment. For the first few days, everything seemed okay, even with the coldness, then one night he announced he was going out with the guys. Ruth objected, and the next thing she knew she was backhanded across the mouth. Alex became violent when he was drunk, and Ruth became the object that he took his aggression out on.

As time went on, Alex went out more and more until he was out late every night, not coming home until early in the morning. If Ruth dared say a word, she would be backhanded or belted. This became a ritual, to the point that all she had to do was anger him, and he would beat her with either his fists or the belt. Ruth did her best to hide the marks from her family, how could she complain? Hadn't she been the one that insisted upon marrying Alex? Did not she essentially make her own bed? Perhaps she deserved this; she was the one that had failed him when she was hospitalized.

Ruth knew that there was no escape, and so she began to blank it out. She would blame herself- *I did not fry his eggs right that is why he picked up the dinner table and threw it across the kitchen.* Or *I did not keep the house cleaned the way he likes it that is why he beat me with the belt and then raped me.* There was not a wealth of self-help groups that a battered woman could go to for help in the 1960's in Watertown, NY. She did what many women did at the time, she accepted her fate. She was married and divorce was not an option. Alex had told her that if she ever left, he would kill her, and that is something she believed he would do. Ruth was a victim of domestic abuse.

CHAPTER TWO

Childhood Memories

What are some of your childhood memories? Do you know what your earliest memories are? How far back can you remember? You may be surprised by what you can remember. Some of those vague memories that we shrug off as things we could not have possibly have remembered, are true memories.

Sarah lived for the first three years with her maternal grandparents, and the memories she had of that time were happy memories. Things like the box of paper dolls that were under the couch, and the small dog that played alongside of her. Her grandfather coming home with dresses and dolls for her, a grandmother that used to rock her and sing to her for hours on end, or the young uncles that used to play with her and get her toys. Sarah had good memories before the age of four.

When Sarah was four years old, Alex and Ruth took their daughter out of the care of her grandparents and brought her to live with them. This is where Sarah's memories began to differ. Memories of her mother crying, her father yelling, and her mother whipped with a belt, and Sarah herself whipped with that same belt. They were eating dinner one night, and Alex decided that Ruth had not made the supper to his liking. He picked up the dinner table and threw it across the room. No one ate dinner that night. Huddled in the corner of the room, Sarah watched as her father viciously beat her mother.

In Sarah's eyes, Alex had two faces, the face of the kind father during the day, the father that would hold her on his knee or play his guitar and sing for her, and then the beast that came out at night, which would hurt her and her mommy. Of course, a four year old does not understand alcoholism and Alex was an alcoholic. Not only did he drink nightly, but also his moods became exceedingly menacing. He was even more aggressive after drinking. Whoever was in his reach ended up as his target for the night, and it did not matter whom it was; the dog, Ruth or Sarah.

In an effort to improve their financial situation, Ruth decided to take a job outside of caring for Sarah. This meant Sarah had to be taken to babysitters. Instead of taking her to her grandmother's, Ruth and Alex decided that an elderly person that they knew from the neighborhood would watch Sarah. Ruth's father had passed away earlier that year and Mary was still grieving. Albert seemed like a reasonable choice. What they did not know was that Albert was a pedophile.

This was when the memories became extremely dark for Sarah. During the day, she would go to Al's, and they would play the games she could not talk about or Mommy and Daddy would die. One time Sarah was crying during the games, and Al covered her head with a pillow and pushed her against the couch holding her still, causing Sarah to develop a fear of being pinned down or laid upon. Ruth and Alex began to notice that Sarah cried when it was time to go to Al's, but they dismissed it, figuring it was just a case of a child not wanting to leave her parents. For six, months they took Sarah to Al's house, never suspecting anything was amiss.

What saved Sarah from Al's constant abuse was a bout of pneumonia. Sarah was hospitalized for almost a month before her fifth birthday. Mercy hospital at that time had few private rooms, and many patients were cared for in wards. Sarah was kept in a crib with a closing top. If the nurses forgot to close the top, Sarah-who hated the crib, would often climb out of it and wander down the hall to where the teenagers were. One of the teenagers on the ward had his guitar and would play it during the day, and Sarah loved to sit and listen to the music. Music was a calming force to Sarah. When she listened to music, the darkness of her daily life was pushed into the background.

Sarah was released from the hospital the day before her 5th birthday. She was extremely happy when her parents walked her down the street from the hospital to her Grandmother's house. The next day she had a spectacular birthday party. All of her cousins and the neighborhood children were invited. Sarah also got the best present in the world, a purple roadrunner. A purple bike with a banana seat and handle bars with sparkle streamers.

It is astounding how children can bounce back from stress, and illness. Sarah was a child who had an extraordinary inner strength and soon the time spent with Albert became nothing but a bad dream to her. Sarah's life was changing. School was on the horizon, her mommy was staying home again, and her parents were no longer mad at her grandmother, which meant that Sarah could spend time with Mary again.

That summer both Alex and Ruth worked at the local fair as carnies. Every day, Sarah would go with them. Her dad worked at a game booth and Ruth sold food at a concession stand. Sarah was allowed to roam around the fair, playing with the other carnie children. Sarah loved the fair, and all it represented; cotton candy, candied apples, and the lights at night. Her favorite ride was the merry-go-round, and when she rode the pony, she dreamed she was in a magical place far away from her reality.

Before school began Ruth and Mary took Sarah shopping, only unlike a lot of the other girls going to kindergarten, Sarah did not go to the department store to shop for clothes. Instead, they went to the Salvation Army. This was fun for Sarah and a place that she was accustomed to shopping for clothes and toys. Remember Alex did not hold a steady job and Ruth was staying home to take care of Sarah, so money was scarce. Sarah was oblivious to their poverty, and picked out what she thought were pretty clothes.

A phrase often said "kids can be cruel" but that is actually an understatement. Sarah will always remember the bus ride home on that first day of school. The other girls on the bus picked on her for her welfare clothes, and her red hair.

Ah, yes... Sarah had red hair, when she was younger; it was as bright as carrots. One thing that kids love to pick on is anything that is different from them. In her kindergarten class, Sarah, with her bright red hair, was the only little girl wearing second hand clothes she was their target, and would remain their target while Sarah attended that school. Every bus trip was the same; they would taunt and tease her, and call her names like stinky and welfare girl. Sarah began to dread going to school.

In 1970, they did not have classrooms for gifted children, and so any child that did not march to the beat of the same drummer, were classified as difficult. Sarah who was always allowed to ask questions at home was suddenly disciplined at school for talking too much.

An incident that still haunts Sarah occurred one rainy day during naptime. As instructed by the teacher, all of the children had to lie down on their blankets and be quiet during naptime. Sarah who was an observant little girl noticed that someone had left their rubber boots on the radiator.

Sarah called out, "Mrs. Jones somebody put their rubber boots on the radiator". The teacher immediately went over to Sarah and scolded her for talking during naptime. "But, Mrs. Jones, the boots are melting" protested Sarah.

Before Sarah realized what was happening, Mrs. Jones had picked her up by the arm and dragged her over to a closet, pushed her in and closed the door.

Sarah who was afraid of the dark immediately became hysterical, crying, begging, and pounding on the door "Please Mrs. Jones please let me out." Sarah continued to bang and pound on the door for a few minutes until the teacher came back. Mrs. Jones who was infuriated with the screaming child pulled open the door, smacked Sarah hard across the face, and taped her mouth shut. "Sarah, do not talk during nap time." The teacher then pushed the child down and closed the door.

Sarah could not tell you how long she was in the closet, but the fear continued to build. When she was finally let out of the dark space, the little girl was broken and sad. Moreover, the episode gave the girls that picked on her even more ammunition. When Sarah got home that day, she begged Ruth not to send her back to school. Ruth held Sarah as she cried, and Sarah finally told her what happened in the classroom. Ruth was furious, and that night when Alex got home she told him what the teacher had done to their daughter.

Instead of becoming mad at the teacher, Alex became angry with Sarah and Ruth. Alex beat Sarah with the belt that night. With each accompanying stroke of the belt, Alex told Sarah that she was disobedient and a disgrace to him. After that night and the beating Alex administered, Sarah realized that you could not tell on adults. Adults were never wrong, only children were wrong. Telling only meant you got hurt more.

Alex got a job in the town of Clayton, and before the school year was out, they moved. Sarah was going to go to school with her cousin Jeffrey Cornaire. Jeffrey was her favorite cousin. One reason for that was because Jeffrey had red hair and freckles like hers, and now she would not be the only one in her class with red hair. Jeffrey and Sarah used to walk to school every day and once again, school became fun for Sarah.

The year was 1970 and the hippie movement did not evade the small town of Clayton. Sarah and Jeffrey would sit in the storefront two doors down from the Cornaire house and listen to the hippies talk. The hippies would smoke from a funny pipe and eventually the guitars would come out and everyone would sing. Those were good times.

One day Sarah and Jeffrey decided to go on an adventure. They were not allowed to leave the block, but both of them disobeyed that day. Their mothers would tell the children to go out and play after lunch so the two women could watch soap operas and not be disturbed. Sarah and Jeffrey decided to go down to the docks that day. Walking down James Street, they made their way past the Bertrand's Hotel, and finally made it to the drugstore on the corner of James and Riverside.

Each child had a quarter, and so they filled their bags with penny candy. After their shopping spree, they crossed Riverside Drive and went to the docks. The rest of the afternoon they watched the ships go up and down the St. Lawrence River and ate their candy. When the two five year olds finally made their way back home, both of their mothers were standing on the porch, holding wooden paddles. They both were spanked that day with the paddles, but neither of the children cared, they had an adventure!

Alex would move where the work was and when the job ended in Clayton, they moved out to a farm in the Dry Hill area. First grade was at Adams Center, and the farm paid good money, enough that Sarah had her first clothes for school from a department store like the other little girls. If clothes could make a girl happy life would have been simple, but with the extra money, Alex also began to drink more.

One night that is still vivid in Sarah's mind was the night that Alex raped Ruth. He came home drunk, and Ruth was angry with him and not in a co-operative mood. Sarah watched as Alex took out the belt, and whipped Ruth. When his arm grew tired, he grabbed Ruth and threw her on the bed, raping her. Sarah who slept in the room with them witnessed the aggression. Ruth would not deny Alex pleasure again, out of fear for her life. Watching her parents have sex became normal for Sarah. It did not take long before Ruth told Alex that she was pregnant, and Alex who was too afraid of Ruth miscarrying, focused on a new target for his abuse. Sarah.

Sarah also began to see "the man" standing at the edge of her bed at night. The man always looked menacing to Sarah and many nights she would wake up screaming at the top of her lungs, and either Alex or Ruth would have to sit with her to get her settled down. Alex tried to convince Sarah that nothing was there, but Sarah knew otherwise, the man, the evil man, was there and always waiting for her.

Sarah used to spend as much time down stairs with the farmer, his wife, and their daughter Nancy, as she was allowed to. Nancy was a year older than Sarah was, but they had become good friends quickly, and Wayva, Nancy's mother tried to protect Sarah by keeping her downstairs as often as possible. However, sometimes there was nothing that could be done; Alex was just in a mood. Maybe Sarah would go to school with a black eye, explained to the teacher that the girl was clumsy, or a cut along her arm, she fell, when actually she was pushed into a pool table, which had a jagged edge. This again was the 70's, and though teachers asked questions, they did not press the issue.

Sometimes when the family downstairs would hear the screams the farmer would go upstairs and take Sarah away from Alex. At other times, they just ignored the screams. Good days were often mixed with bad days, and Sarah never knew what type of day it would become. One night when her father was spanking her, Sarah decided that she was not going to cry anymore. The six year old realized that her tears seemed to make Alex happy and so closing her mind to the pain she squelched her tears that night and refused to cry for him anymore. It was the only way a six year old could have some sort of control over her circumstances. Sarah had obtained a minor victory; not crying meant she was in control.

CHAPTER THREE

From the Frying Pan into the Fire

The winter of 72 brought with it a lot of snow. Sunday's meant a trip to Watertown to Mary's house for dinner. This Sunday though the weather was miserable, despite the warning from the farmer and his wife Alex decided to head to town anyways. The unplowed road was slippery which made the drive even more hazardous than normal. Alex only had one speed when he drove, and that was fast. The truck sped down Dry Hill, and both Ruth and Sarah were already afraid. Their fear turned into terror as they saw a snow plow approach them heading up the hill, both wings out, Alex was going too fast, he could not stop. Alex swung the steering wheel to try to avoid the plow. The truck they were in, crashed through the rail, and went over the side of the hill. Ruth was thrown out of the truck, and Alex held Sarah in with his arm as the truck rolled three times. It was a miracle that any of them survived.

Ruth ended up going into labor a few days later, and Scott would be born a month early, February 19, 1972. Scott was born prematurely due to the car accident that the family was in, but despite that, he was a healthy baby boy, the pride of Alex, who finally got his son. Sarah loved her new baby brother. To Sarah he was almost as good as getting a doll to play with, and she enjoyed helping Ruth out with the baby.

When things are downright bad in your life, have you ever thought that they could not get any worse? Alternatively, have you heard the phrase "They jumped from the frying pan right into the fire"? Turning seven was a turning point in Sarah's life.

Sometimes when Alex went out, Ruth would accompany him to the bars, and one night while they were, out she met a woman named Marie.

The two women struck up a friendship and soon Marie was spending a lot of time at the house with Ruth and Alex. Marie had a daughter named Elizabeth. Liz and Sarah used to spend a lot of time playing together, even though Liz was only four and Sarah was seven. It was difficult to communicate with Liz because she was deaf, but the girls developed a language.

When Marie was around, Alex did not hit Ruth or Sarah, and for a while, it seemed that life was getting better. The adults began talking about a place called California and jobs there and better weather. Soon the talks became reality. Alex and Ruth packed up everything they had, attached a U-Haul to the back of their car and the three adults and three children started the cross-country trip to California.

The trip across the country was endless to a seven year old, and Sarah who was known for her finicky eating habits soon would stretch the limits of her parents. The only way for Sarah to have any control during the trip was to decide what she did or did not eat. Try finding grilled cheese sandwiches and French fries for breakfast, lunch, and dinner. Alex and Ruth decided that their best options were truck stops, and that is where they ate for eleven days straight. Imagine a trip across the country with two young children and a six-month-old baby. You probably do not have all of the money that you need, so you stop along the way and find an odd job here and there, enough to get some food and fuel and get back on the road again.

It was in the Mojave Desert when the station wagon gave its final breath and died. In 1972, there was one gas station at the beginning of the Mojave, one in the middle and one just at the other end. Of course, their car did not break down at any of those gas stations, and the three adults had to make a decision. The two women would try to thumb a ride with the children and Alex would stay with the car and U-Haul. A truck driver came by and agreed to take the two women and children to the gas station in the middle of the desert. Once there Ruth and Marie would send a tow truck back for Alex.

Sarah remembers sitting around a fire that night, watching some weird bugs dance (scorpions). An old Indian man told a story while they waited for her father to get there. Once there they got the distressing news, the car was beyond repair. Alex had to sell everything in the U-Haul to get enough money to buy bus tickets for them to get the rest of the way to California. That meant that everything Sarah owned was sold, including her prized purple roadrunner.

On day eleven, they finally arrived in Fresno California and were picked up at the Greyhound bus station by a woman named Wanda and her husband Bill. They all went back to Wanda and Bills house, which was a two-bedroom apartment where five adults and six children were now going to live.

Things immediately began to get strange, especially when the women announced that they were going to sleep in the main bed, and the men could sleep out in the living room. Until that point in time, Alex did not know that Marie was a lesbian and that Ruth and Marie had been having an affair for several months before leaving for California. Alex was not happy but did not dare take out his anger on Ruth when others were around.

Bill who was a trucker went out on the road for a delivery, leaving the women alone with Alex. Alex, angry with Ruth about her sexual preferences, got quite drunk one night. He went into the bedroom where the children slept and took Sarah into the living room with him. He put his hands under her nightgown feeling her, and Sarah began trying to push herself away from him. He was too strong, clamping his hand firmly over her mouth so she could not scream. She cried silently into his hand, the scent of alcohol heavy on his breath. She felt him press up against her back, then thrust repeatedly. When he was done with her, he cleaned her up and warned her that if she ever told anyone about what happened he would have to go away.

A few mornings later Alex and Scott were missing. Sarah remembers going into the bedroom crying to herself, whispering "but I did

not tell anyone daddy why did you go away".
Alex had left Ruth, and hitch hiked back to New
York with his six month old son Scott, leaving
Sarah with her mother and Marie.

With Alex out of the picture, Marie began to
take over child care of Sarah. Sarah who had
been allowed to bathe herself suddenly was told
she was no longer able to give herself a bath, and
Marie would come in nightly to bathe Sarah. Her
finger probing the young girl, explaining as she
did, "You need to be clean everywhere." Around
this time, Marie also began disciplining Sarah;
this would include locking her in a closet or
whipping her with a belt.

Visions of "the man" became a common
occurrence for Sarah, and she would beg for the
light to remain on her room. Marie and Ruth
finally bought a nightlight for Sarah's room to
try to quiet the seven year old. Sarah also began
to have recurring dreams that started at the age
of seven until she was seventeen. These dreams
were of her being kidnapped and kept as a toy
for the people that took her. Sarah did not know

what the dreams meant, but it was not uncommon for her to experience this dream several times a week, each time she woke up she was terrified, and would lie in her bed trembling.

It was at age seven that Sarah also began to develop migraine headaches so severe that the pain would bring her to her knees, and the child would lie on the floor holding her head, or vomit from the pressure of the migraine. Marie who felt these migraines were manipulations would whip Sarah with the belt and send her to the room. Sarah was not taken to the doctors for the migraines, but instead whipped.

If Ruth tried to interfere with Marie when she was disciplining Sarah, Marie would lash out at Ruth, beating her savagely. There was no hope for Sarah, she just had to endure, and in order to endure she began to become detached during the beatings. She would watch as a spectator as a little girl was beat, but in her mind, she was not that little girl.

At the end of second grade, the adults announced that they were heading back to New York and would attempt to get custody of baby Scott. This was the best news for Sarah who desperately missed her grandmother and uncles and was hoping that when they got to New York her mother and father would get back together and Marie would go away. This was not going to be a wish that came true for Sarah.

Ruth did regain custody of Scott and retrieved him out of a foster home, where Alex had eventually left his son before leaving the country and going to Montreal Canada to work at his uncles shoe store.

Ruth, who was afraid of Marie, did not tell her family about the beatings, instead portrayed Marie as someone that she loved, and someone who took care of her. Instead of being a loving partner, Marie began to take over the abuse where Alex left off, the only difference is Marie was not doing it because she was drunk – she did it because she was a sadist, and Ruth was essentially her slave.

Marie also did not care for males, and Scott was a male, even though he was only two years old. Marie began to take frustrations out on the toddler, keeping him in a playpen all day because he was too much of a hassle to watch, taping his mouth shut with duct tape if he cried, and making him sleep at night tied to bed so he would not get out. Sarah quietly watched these things happen to her little brother but did not tell anyone because she knew you only got in trouble when you told on adults.

Life was not all grim, and from an outsiders view Sarah looked like the typical child growing up in upstate New York. Weekdays during the summer were spent playing outside with other children at the playground. Back in the 70's money was allocated to public playgrounds, and these playgrounds had recreational staff. These playgrounds essentially provided daycare for the neighborhood children during the day. Parents would drop their children off in the morning and pick them up in the late afternoon. Sarah enjoyed the summers the best, being outside with other children, participating in sports, arts and crafts, summer time was the time of escape. Once the playgrounds closed down Sarah had to spend her days in the house, and it was in the house with Marie that Sarah hated being.

When Sarah was nine years old, her family moved to the city of Carthage. Marie worked at the St. Regis Paper Mill and it was easier for her to commute to work from Carthage than it was in Watertown. For Sarah, this would be the sixth school that she would attend. Sarah was in 3rd grade and due to the constant school changes, the once bright student began faltering in reading. She had attended three different schools in the second grade, and despite her best efforts to keep up, she was falling behind.

In school, there are good teachers and incompetent teachers, and that year Sarah ended up with a bad teacher, Mrs. Smith. Mrs. Smith could not be bothered with a child that struggled and so she devoted her time to the students that were achieving. Sarah was classified as a child that was lazy and careless, and whenever the opportunity arose, Mrs. Smith seized that moment to discipline Sarah in some way. Perhaps it would be missing recess, or sitting in the corner for the day because she could not read a passage.

When angry, Mrs. Smith was not beyond physical discipline and Sarah remembers being pulled out of the room once by her braids. Why... because a boy had kissed her and she did not like it and slapped him across the face. Mrs. Smith ended up dragging her down the hall by the hair of her head to the Principal's office. The Principal talked to Sarah and told her it was not appropriate to hit someone, even if they did kiss her.

The principal told Sarah "Someday you will like boys kissing you." Sarah doubted that. She begged the Principal not to tell her mother, but the principal made the call home, and Marie came and picked up Sarah at school.

Sarah was terrified of what would happen because she knew Marie did not like to be called by the school. Sarah was made to stand with her pants to her ankles that night while Marie used a wooden board on her, repeatedly. Sarah lost count of how many times she was hit. Marie was hoping to get the girl to cry but Sarah was still holding in her tears. At the end of the night, despite being covered in welts and blisters, not one tear was shed until she was in her room alone.

The beating was so severe that Sarah could not sit down properly for almost a week; the blisters swelled up and filled with fluid. The blisters were so bad that Marie became afraid, and called a friend of hers who Sarah referred to as Grandpa Jake. Grandpa Jake had helped when Sarah was sick a few times before. Once when she had a bad case of the croup, he made some honey and onion cough syrup for her. This time, he made a milk poultice and layered it on her bottom until the blisters popped. Sarah who was in agony just cried and cried, Grandpa Jake ran his fingers through her hair, trying to soothe while he treated her. She heard him reprimand

Marie for hitting the child too hard. Finally, Sarah was able to go back to school, but the damage was done. Missing the week of school only made Sarah get farther behind.

The abuse on Scott continued to grow day by day. The 3-year-old toddler was essentially tied by a rope with a collar on his neck during the day. The explanation of it was to keep him out of things. He was not allowed to eat at the table, his plate was put on the floor, and he had to eat with his hands. Again, an explanation was readily available; he just could not seem to learn how to use a spoon, so it was easier that way. One time Scott pulled his dirty diaper off and spread the poop on the walls. When Marie found him playing with the poop, she took handful after handful and shoved it into the toddlers' mouth, making him eat it. Scott was diagnosed with ADD at the local head start, and this diagnosis seemed to be an excuse for all of the discipline that began to be rained down on the toddler.

One night Sarah had an idea, maybe if she used the phone she could call for help, a brave act for a 10 year old but something she needed to do. Not knowing whom to call she dialed "0" for the operator. When the operator came on line, Sarah spoke in whispers, "Please can you send the police, my brother and I are being hurt, we need help, please get us help," and then she hung up the phone. Instead of calling the police, the operator called the house number, and when Marie answered the phone, she was told by the operator that it seemed that someone was calling for help from that number, did she know anything about it? Marie apologized and said it must be kids making prank calls.

This created another memory in Sarah's mind that adults could not be trusted to help you when you asked for help. That night she was beaten for using the phone without permission, and trying to get her family in trouble. Sarah began to realize that no one was going to help her; she just had to figure out a way to endure whatever Marie decided to do to her.

Shortly after her 10th birthday, Marie informed Sarah that she was going to go and stay with some friends of hers. She was given strict instructions on how she should behave and that she should obey unconditionally. She was going to be staying there for the weekend, and so some clothes were packed for her. When she got there, she found out that she was going to be staying with two women. Sarah thought it was strange that they did not have any children, but they did have dogs.

Sarah enjoyed her day there as she was allowed to be out in their big yard playing with the dogs. While she played, she pretended that she was rescued from the evil Marie, and the two women, Jane and Wendy, were going to keep her safe forever and ever. It was a lovely day; they even made her grilled cheese and French fries. She did not much like the drink they called grape juice, she thought it tasted funny. The "grape juice" was actually wine, and they insisted that she drink two full glasses of it.

After dinner they took her into their bedroom and removed her clothes, Sarah became afraid... "Quiet" Jane whispered in her ear, kissing the girls forehead, "be a good girl now, you do not want me to tell Marie and your mother that you were disobedient do you?" Sarah who was drunk stopped struggling and let the women touch her that night. She was such a good girl that they requested her again and again, and she spent many weekends at their house, it was always the same, daytime she could play on her own, and at nighttime she was the toy – the plaything for two adult lesbians.

Despite the sexual abuse that was taking place, Sarah actually preferred the weekends that she was with Wendy. They were at least kind to her. If she was at home with Marie and her mother, she knew that she would experience the belt of Marie or have to undergo one of the baths, which Sarah hated. Sarah did not know it, but these abuses were grooming her for years and years of steady abuse. Things that would seem like an atrocity to others were the norm for Sarah. She thought that every little girl went away to special aunts on the weekend, and that little brothers with ADD were tied up because that is how you teach them to sit still.

CHAPTER FOUR

The Plaything Begins to Ask Questions

Sarah's behavior at Wendy and Jane's always resulted in glowing reports to Marie and her mother, so much so that Marie decided that she should lend Sarah out to another couple that she knew. Though actual money was not exchanged, a weekend with the girl would result in some repair of the house, or help with an errand. Sarah became an object that Marie could barter for the things that she needed.

In Marie's eyes, she owned Ruth, and since Sarah was Ruth's daughter that also meant she owned Sarah. A 10 year old does not actually have an understanding of what an object is, but Sarah felt emptiness inside of herself. She knew she was different from other little girls at school, she knew that they did not all get given to "aunts" for the weekend. Most of the girls at school talked about their weekends, what they did with their families, shopping trips, sleepovers. Sarah used to sit and listen to them but did not dare join in. She also suspected that other little girls did not have things put inside of them. Marie, Wendy and Jane, would put things inside of Sarah; fingers, a small bottle, something long and smooth. She knew her sleepovers were not quite the same as theirs, and she knew she could not tell anyone about it.

Fifth grade signified another move and another school change for Sarah. This time they moved from Carthage to Felts Mills, and Sarah was going to attend the school called Great Bend Elementary. Fifth grade was a lot of fun, and Sarah's teacher Mrs. Jewett helped Sarah get caught up in reading and math.

Moving to Felts Mills also meant more children; there were the Browns on one side, and the Mack's on the other. The Browns had four children including Jimmy who was a year older than Sarah was and Patty who was a year younger than Sarah was. The Mack's had three children, one of the girls whose name was Jane, was the same age as Sarah. The group of kids hung out all the time together.

The road that they lived on was called the Cemetery Road, which was, at that time, a dirt road. This road afforded many "fun" opportunities for the kids that lived there. Bikes were brought out in the summer and the kids would race up and down the road, the dirt flying all around them with the wind in their hair. When it got too hot, they could always stop and take a quick trek through the woods to the creek – which was always cold-to go wading.

It was while wading at that creek that Sarah got her first kiss from Jimmy, and he asked her to be his girlfriend. Jimmy was the oldest and best-looking boy on the street, so Sarah immediately said yes. Marie of course had a fit of anger when she heard that Sarah was kissing boys in the woods, and called her a slut. That night she informed her if she kept kissing the boy, she was going to be pregnant. When the following weekend rolled around Sarah was not allowed to go out to play, she was grounded for having a boyfriend. After that weekend when Jimmy tried to kiss Sarah – she would push him away and say, "I cannot be your girlfriend." An innocent romance was twisted into something dirty, and Sarah was ashamed.

Marie's daughter Elizabeth was deaf, and though she was with the family on the weekends, during the week she went to school at a place called Rome State School for the Deaf. Every Sunday they would drop Liz off, and every Friday Liz would come home. Liz was being taught sign language at school, and she taught Sarah how to sign so that they could talk with one another.

Because Liz was deaf, Marie said that she could not be spanked when she was bad, so Liz quickly learned that she could get away with just about anything and blame it either on Scott or Sarah.

Scott who was four years old now spent most of his days after head start bound to a chair, blindfolded and gagged. Marie explained that tying him to a chair was teaching him to sit still. That blindfolding him kept him from being distracted, and gagging him taught him not to talk uncontrollably. Marie took every opportunity to walk by the boy and slap him or if he was bound on the floor, to kick him.

One night Sarah watched as Marie went into a fit and broke a dish over the little boy's head, blood pouring down his face. That night Ruth finally stood up for her son, but it did no good. Marie tackled Ruth to the floor, beating on her as she did, putting a knife to Ruth's throat she threatened to kill her if she went to the authorities.

Until that night, Sarah had not realized the extent of the abuse that her mother was also enduring at the hands of Marie. Ruth was literally scared for her life, and afraid of being alone. At least Marie provided them with a home, and nice things. She was too afraid of leaving the "things," and the thought of going back to Alex was less than appealing to Ruth. Besides at this point Alex had a 15-year-old girlfriend that he was going to marry, getting back with him was no longer an option.

It was at school one day that Sarah got educated on what a lesbian was and that her mother was a lesbian. This brought shame to Sarah, and she hated being made fun of by the kids. She also began to question if she was a lesbian, as she was still being lent out to Marie's friends on a regular basis, and Marie would not let her be Jimmy's boyfriend. Sarah hated this possibility more than anything; she hated the thought that she might be a lesbian too.

This caused Sarah to play with the boys more than the girls the following summer, playing tackle football, and hiding in forts, letting the boys tie her up when they played Cowboys and Indians or the Kidnapper game.

Much to her dismay, at around eleven Sarah's body began to change, and now the boys started acting weird around her. When they were alone playing, the boys would say "Pull up your shirt so we can see your boobies" Sarah who was used to people looking and touching her, did not even hesitate but would pull up her shirt, laugh and run off. One of the boys was overheard talking by his parents, and they immediately went to Ruth and said Sarah is a detrimental influence on our boys, she keeps lifting up her shirt.

Ruth was of course mortified at Sarah's behavior, and when Sarah came home that day, she was greeted with a slap across the face and called a "whore" by Ruth, who told her she was going to become a tramp and get pregnant if she insisted on hanging out with the boys. Something snapped in Sarah, and she yelled back at her mother, "Am I a whore when your friends take my clothes off and touch me, am I a whore when Marie gives me a bath"? Ruth looked at her daughter with a blank stare and said, "Go to your room, and never repeat such things again." Sarah went to her room, slamming the door, and cried herself to sleep that night. Her mother was not going to do anything to stop what was happening, she was not even sure that her mother believed her. This was yet again another time when Sarah tried to fight back, only to find that not a single adult was going to help her.

CHAPTER FIVE

New Friends & Life Changes

When Sarah was twelve the family, if that is what you want to refer to it as, moved, back to the city of Watertown. They went from their remote trailer in Felts Mills to an apartment building on 122 Ten Eyck Street. Compared to the house that they lived in before, this place was a dump and small. Sarah had to go back to sharing a room with Liz, which was not so miserable because Liz was at school all week in Rome. Scott had a mattress on the floor in the hallway and Marie, and Ruth had their room.

There were some good things though about being back in Watertown. They were once again close enough to Sarah's grandmother so that she could see her on a regular basis, and the apartment building was filled with kids. One of those kids was named Sandy.

Sandy was the same age as Sarah, and they became friends almost immediately. Sandy lived in the apartment under Sarah. Sandy had two older brothers' one named Luis who was 16 and another that was 21 his name was Patrick. Sandy also had a sister named Joanna, but Joanna did not live there with them, she was in college and engaged soon to be married. Sarah immediately developed a crush on the brothers, Luis was dreamy, and Patrick was a musician.

Patrick sang and played the guitar and in the eyes of an impressionable 13 year old – Patrick was "cool." Patrick was off limits though, he was married. Therefore, instead of focusing on Patrick, Sarah set her sights on Luis, who considered her nothing more than a stupid kid and made it his business to ignore her.

That was also the year that Scott entered kindergarten, and unlike the head start teachers that ignored the boys bruises, his kindergarten teacher noticed and filed a report with the child protective agency. Ruth and Marie were called; someone was coming to the house to interview them. Marie told Sarah what to say, and instructed Ruth on what she was allowed to say. Both mother and daughter were terrified of what would happen if they disobeyed.

A caseworker came to the home as scheduled and interviewed the children, though both children had been coached to deny any abuse, the caseworker made the recommendation to remove Scott from the house. Alex was given the opportunity to take his five-year-old son back; he had just married his second wife and was expecting their first child. Sarah watched as her brother was rescued, but once again, she was left there, once again in the eyes of Sarah her father was leaving her alone. Once again, no one rescued Sarah.

Sarah and Sandy became the best of friends, and it was through Sandy that Sarah learned that things were not quite right in her life. Sandy was shocked when Sarah explained one night that she was not allowed to take a bath alone and that Marie always gave her a bath. Sandy said, "Why do not you just take a shower and lock the bathroom door"? Sarah did not answer Sandy, but knew if she dared to try that, Marie would beat her. She just merely said "ok" to Sandy, and the subject was dropped.

Soon after they moved in, Patrick approached Ruth and Marie. His wife with whom he was estranged from wanted to move in with him, and they wanted to work on their relationship. They had a newborn baby and had no place to stay. Marie and Ruth said they could stay there, and they moved in, Patrick, his wife Corey and their baby boy Peter, moved in and this afforded a reprieve for Sarah.

Marie was too worried about someone seeing what she did to Sarah, so at that time the sexual abuse ended. Sarah was no longer supervised during baths, and for a while, even some of the physical abuse stopped. Patrick and Corey broke up again, yet Patrick remained at the apartment with Marie and Ruth. Sarah did not know it at the time, but Patrick and Ruth had gotten involved with one another. This was short lived, and Patrick eventually moved out, but Ruth was through being a lesbian and a man named Danny soon moved in.

It was around this time that talk about California started up again. One day they packed up what they owned, and the three adults and two children (Sarah and Liz) got into the station wagon. They drove across the United States for the second time in Sarah's life, although this time the trip only took five days.

It was in California that Ruth finally got the courage to leave Marie. Danny and Ruth got an apartment with Sarah, and for once in Sarah's life, things were finally looking up. Danny was fantastic; she immediately started calling him Dad. Danny did not yell at her, he did not hit her, or molest her; he treated her like a princess. Ruth was happier now than she had been in years, and Sarah began to experience childhood without fear.

She had a budding romance at school with a boy named Mike; and Danny and Ruth even allowed her to go out on dates to the roller rink with him. The thing that was most beneficial during this time is that Sarah found a sense of happiness in church. She went to a church called Bakersfield Baptist church every. One Sunday in particular, when the preacher asked the sinners to come forward Sarah went up to the front of the Church with tears streaming down her face and said softly, "Pastor Ledbetter, I want to be saved." That day Sarah accepted Jesus as her savior and Sarah was convinced that nothing harmful was ever going to happen to her again, and for a while, it seemed that way.

About mid-way through eighth grade, Danny and Ruth decided that they needed to move back to New York, Danny could not find a job in Fresno, but he had a friend in Watertown that would give him a job when he got there. Not having much money, they sold what they owned, and headed back across the US.

To help alleviate some costs they picked up a hitchhiker along the way. To Sarah this guy was very cool, he had long hair, wore bell bottoms like the guys from the Monkeys did, and he listened to "swell" music. He stayed with the family until their car broke down outside of Memphis. Danny, Ruth, and Sarah got on a Greyhound bus to Memphis and spent the night in a shelter there while waiting for money to be wired from Sarah's grandmother to get them the rest of the way home. One of the things that Sarah fondly remembers of that day was getting to see the outside of the Grand Ole Opry before they boarded the bus. Two days later, they were back in Watertown and were going to live with Sarah's grandmother.

The first thing that Sarah did was find a church that she could go to in Watertown. The Ledbetter's had recommended a church called Watertown Baptist Temple. Much to Sarah's dismay Ruth and Danny broke up shortly after they got back to Watertown and Sarah felt a considerable loss in her life. She had just lost a man that was a genuine father figure and one that had no hidden agenda.

Though Sandy and Sarah were not living in the same apartment building anymore, the girls remained friends and went to the same junior high school, Case Junior. Both would ride their bikes the 10 – 12 blocks to see one another. Sandy still lived on Ten Eyck Street at the time, and Sarah was living on Stone Street. The distance did not stop the girls, sometimes Sandy thought that Sarah was a little too religious for her, but they were friends despite Sarah's need for religion.

At this time, Sarah became highly active in the church and spent a lot of time out with the Pastor and his family. Pastor Dale knew that Sarah and her mom were living with her grandmother and two uncles in a three-bedroom house, so they invited Sarah to their house whenever they could. Besides helping the teenage girl, Sarah was great with their two young children and the help was a godsend to Nancy. Sarah, who had matured early, was a teenager in a woman's body. The young men at church often did not realize that the mature woman that they thought they were talking to was a thirteen-year-old girl. This gave Pastor

Dale a great deal of indigestion until he decided that if one of his parishioners wanted to date the young girl, the young man would take her out for dinner and he and his wife would be their chaperones. This became sort of a joke in church because a potential suitor had to be able to afford taking three people out on a date, not just one.

It is not uncommon for children of abuse to be abused by many in their lives, and often times they are left wondering, is there a sign up over my head that says abuse me or something? The answer to that is yes, actually, there is. There is something that is broken in the children that make them vulnerable and susceptible to abuse by others, and in some ways, they become a temptation to people, to abuse them.

Sarah went to her Cousin Darlene's house one weekend, to spend the night and hang out with Darlene. While there, Darlene's stepfather Alan gave the two girls wine, and while the two girls were in bed, Alan came in and touched the girls. Later it would be exposed that Alan had been sleeping with his daughter for many years, and though he did not rape Sarah, his touching brought back all of the memories that she thought she was saved from.

She went to Pastor Dale's the following weekend and told him what Uncle Alan had done. Pastor Dale admonished her for drinking and explained to her that liquor would lead her down a path of unrighteousness. That she would become a tramp if she continued down this path. Later that night when Pastor Dale came up to the guest room to tuck her in, he was looking at her differently, contemplating, and instead of kissing her on the forward like he usually did, he pressed his lips against hers almost in a bruising manner and kissed her. After that night, Pastor Dale did not invite her to his home to stay anymore. Sarah thought it was because she drank alcohol and was going to grow up to be a tramp.

Another incident happened while at the church and this one involved two younger women. Sarah used to go out regularly to the Purdy farm to help with the chores. She was friends with Nancy and Richard Purdy and enjoyed the opportunity to earn a little money while working outside. One weekend there were two girls that were at the farm and they were lesbians; the Purdie's were trying to help them.

When one of the women approached Sarah and propositioned her, Sarah started screaming uncontrollably that she was "Not a lesbian and they better not touch her." After that, the Purdies were worried about having Sarah over. They were concerned that she might be emotionally unstable. They had no idea of the abuses that Sarah had gone through for years at the hands of Marie and her friends, and that was why Sarah was hysterical.

Shortly after that Sarah stopped going to church, the clean feeling that she once had while attending had gone away. She started to feel like she did when she was a young kid again. Her mother noticed her depression, took her to the family doctor, and asked that he examine her.

The doctor said, "Sure, Mom, but you need to step out of the room." This was the first time that the pediatrician abused Sarah, and it would not be the last. That day he made her take off all of her clothes, and after a pelvic exam, he said, "You are not a virgin, are you"? This would be one of many visits that Sarah would have to endure.

Ruth, always at the doctor's command, sat out in the waiting room. The routine was always the same, he would tell her to take off all her clothes, he would feel her up, and then look in her throat or ears. He would declare that she had tonsillitis or strep throat, and would say here is some medicine; see you in a few weeks. The doctor said he did not believe in removing tonsils. An outsider might suspect that he much rather preferred to see the young girl on a monthly basis, which he could not do if she was healthy.

She lost her safety in the church, and she lost the safety of an adult that should have been someone Sarah could talk to about her abuse –

instead he too, became an abuser. She was lost, alone and not knowing it at the time, suicidal.

One day Sarah wrote a poem to her eighth grade teacher, Ms. Sammond. In Sarah's eyes, Ms. Sammond was amazing, bright, funny, and remarkably pretty. The poem was about a girl that was sad who decided that no one would notice if the girl disappeared and drowned herself in the Black River.

Sarah did not sign the note but Ms. Simmonds recognized the handwriting and approached Sarah, asking her if she wrote it, and if she wanted to die. Sarah thought for a few moments looked at her teacher and said quite simply "Yes, I do." Though Sarah had never voiced it until that time, she finally realized she did want to die, life was horrible, and there was not much hope that it was going to get any better. The teacher reported this to the school authorities, and a caseworker was assigned.

Ruth was furious with Sarah, furious with her for stirring things up from the past, and when the caseworker came and interviewed Ruth; she lied, and said... "Sarah has a particularly vivid imagination and makes things up; she has never been abused by anyone." For some reason, the caseworker believed Ruth, and that was the end of the investigation. Sarah received some mandated counseling, but not trusting anyone she did not open up to the counselor and divulge what her life had been like, they later dismissed her depression as typical adolescence and she stopped going to a counselor in a few months.

Life went back to normal if you can call it that. Ruth dated one guy after another. Sometimes the guys were personable, other times they were creeps, and they tried to feel Sarah up. After a few months, Ruth announced she was pregnant. They packed their things and moved in with the father of Ruth's unborn child, Steve.

Sarah hated Steve and did not hesitate to tell him so. He would be with them for the next three years. Why did Sarah hate him so much? Sarah hated him because he was a drunk, an alcoholic. He drank away all of their money, he got stupid when he got drunk, he also on occasion would walk into the bathroom when Sarah was there, leering at her. However, this was not the same Sarah that complacently took the abuse in stride; this was a rebellious teenager that fought back.

After Ruth delivered the baby, a boy named Alan, Steve and Ruth would spend less and less time at the apartment with Sarah. In fact, many times they would be at Ruth's mother's house, where there was food and heat, leaving Sarah in a house with little and at times no food.

They lived too far for Sarah to walk to her grandmothers, and it was too far for her to get from her grandmothers to school. Thankfully some neighbors saw that the girl was alone most of the time and took her into their home.

If it were not for the Reeds' and the Reasoners' taking Sarah in and feeding her, Sarah might have starved or worse yet, been arrested for shoplifting. One time she tried to steal food from the State Street A&P and she was caught. The store manager said he never wanted to see her in the store again. It was the Reeds that took her to Faith Fellowship Christian Church. It was there that Sarah once again began to feel that there was some hope in life and perhaps, just perhaps, she could be clean again.

Many families there reached out to her. The names are endless, and kindnesses were innumerable. Sarah learned that she was loved and loveable. She learned to trust again, though she decided she was not going to tell anyone about her past. The best thing in all of this was her friend Sandy finally came to church with her and was born again too. In fact, one after another of Sandy's family was joining the church. This was the best thing in the world as far as Sarah was concerned. Another thing that made her happy was that Steve and Ruth moved from outer State Street back to Watertown, and ironically to 122 Ten Eyck Street.

At first, Sarah was terrified to move back into that building, but she found out that Sandy only lived three blocks away and the dread was overshadowed with the joy of being close to her best friend again. Sarah did not mind now when Steve and Ruth would leave her alone, she would go over to Sandy's house and stay there. It was the summer of 1981, the girls were both respectively turning 16, and life itself was full of adventure.

CHAPTER SIX

Summer of First Love

Sarah had always envisioned what a Sweet 16 birthday party might be like, but in her vision, she never thought she would spend the day alone, no cake, no card, no present. That was, however, her 16th birthday. Sarah sat alone that night in the apartment, imagining what it might be like if she was another girl, in a family that loved her. Would she have a big sweet sixteen party? Would she dance with boys? Would she get many presents. She cried herself to sleep that night.

The pain that she felt that night did not matter for long though because it was the summer of 1981 and Sarah was in love. Of course, she did not have the courage to tell anyone about it yet, she certainly could not tell the man... yes... the man... Sandy's older brother Patrick was now 24 and Sarah, had a HUGE crush on him.

Patrick was living with Sandy and his mother on Flower Avenue, so Sarah had an opportunity to see him daily. Patrick drove a cab at the time, sometimes the two girls would wander down to the Yellow Cab dispatch, and Patrick would give them a ride if they needed one.

He treated her like his little sister, which infuriated Sarah to no end. She would throw things at him, even poke him, anything to irritate him enough that he might tackle or wrestle her down to the ground, sitting on top of her he typically would growl, "knock it off," then get up, and walk away. Other times, he would tickle her until she screamed for him to stop.

One time he tackled her, and it was different... He gazed down at her and did not growl, he actually did not say anything at all. For a moment, she caught his gaze and her eyes must have said... "Kiss me you fool" because that is what her heart was screaming. He of course did not kiss her; he rolled off her, and began to avoid her.

Sarah thought that perhaps she was not pretty enough, that is why he did not kiss her. On the other hand, perhaps he thought she was stupid. She did not fully understand all of the pent up feelings she had when Patrick was around. When he avoided her, it made it even worse.

Sandy began to notice something was going on between Sarah and Patrick and so she went over to Sarah's apartment and said, "What is up between you and my brother"? Sarah, said, "Well it's simple, I love him, and he hates me". She never thought she was going to share this crush with Sandy, but she did, and the two girls talked for hours.

Sarah swore Sandy to secrecy; however, Sarah did not know that keeping a secret was a hard thing for Sandy. Later, Patrick said to Sandy "Why does Sarah have to act stupid" and Sandy blurted out "Because she loves you."

Sarah was at church that night when Sandy came in through the back door and said "Sarah you have to come with me now. While they were walking outside Sandy whispered, "Please do not be mad at me, but I told Patrick. He loves you too and he wants to talk to you."

Sarah was startled, shocked, and in typical 16 year old fashion she wanted to strangle her friend. Instead, she followed Sandy to the car where Patrick was waiting. They drove up to Thompson Park together and parked at Pinnacle Point. Sarah and Patrick sat on the wall and talked and as it turned, out he loved her too, but did not know if he should act upon it. There were several reasons, one, he had an affair with Ruth four years prior. Two, he was eight years older than Sarah was, and of course the main reason was that Sarah was a minor.

Sara confessed her feelings for Patrick, told him that she had loved him since she was thirteen years old. He looked a little confused, but she went on to explain that she had always had a crush on him, but now it was not a crush. She did love him, and yes, she knew what love was about.

They talked for a few hours and established ground rules for their relationship, no sex – Sarah was a minor but besides that Patrick and Sarah were committed to serving God, and they felt that sex outside of marriage was wrong. They would not spend considerable amounts of time alone, either Luis, Sandy or their mom would be around, and they would not hide their relationship. Sandy also started dating a guy that Patrick worked with and so the four would often spend time together, working, singing, and talking about God.

For Sarah it was one of the best summers of her life. For the first time, Sarah was loved for herself, not what she could give sexually, but for who she was. For a child growing up in constant abuse this type of love is a rare find, and when it does happen, it is not always recognized. Patrick thought she was pretty, he did not tell her to be quiet when she talked or acted bored, and the two talked for hours on end, about anything and everything.

They saw each other daily for two months, and they talked about many things, marriage, their future, likes, dislikes. There was no doubt, in either of their minds, that in two years they would get married. Unfortunately, for Sarah, people at the Church became worried with the relationship and both Patrick and Sarah were sat down separately and talked to.

Patrick was given a lecture about his age, and the fact that his divorce from his first wife was not final. What was he thinking dating a girl that was only 16 years old? He needed to submit to God and end the relationship.

For Sarah, the conversation went quite a bit differently. Sarah you and Patrick are having sex, do you want to become a tramp, or a woman of God? Sarah vehemently denied having sex with Patrick. She had not; he would not have sex with her even when she tried to get him to. However, no one would listen to her; they just kept at her telling her how bad she was, and that the relationship had to end. After a few hours, Sarah stormed out of the room, telling everyone there to go to hell. She had no idea that Patrick had already agreed to end the relationship.

The next morning Patrick told her he could no longer date her that he wanted to do right and follow what leadership had commanded. Sarah was in shock, and hurt. She refused to go back to church, even when Sandy and some other friends asked her to. The pain of being referred to as a tramp was too great for Sarah she did not understand why no one believed her about not having sex.

In the past, she had always fought to prove people wrong, but now she had given up. The one person that she loved was taken away from her. The one pure relationship in her life gone and she decided there was no longer a reason to fight her destiny.

CHAPTER SEVEN

Rescue Comes Strangely Packaged

Age 16 to 17 became a blur as Sarah used alcohol as a means to escape the pain and betrayal she felt. Steve had finally moved out, and Sarah, Ruth, and her little brother Alan, were living at the East Hills housing project. Alcohol was easy to come by; in fact, Ruth would purchase it for Sarah. Sex became something that Sarah became infatuated with. At 17, she began to throw herself at everyone – still there were not any takers, and it was not because Sarah was not attractive, she was.

Finally, she found someone, a brother of one of the women that she used to go to church with. His name was Chip, and he was 32 years old. Sarah had met Chip a few years back and would run into him every now and then at the State Street McDonalds. One day they saw each other, and Chip said, "Hey why do not you come on in and get some coffee with me," they talked for a while, and Sarah finally got up the nerve to pop the question, "Chip, will you have sex with me"?

Chip almost spilled his coffee and looked at the 17-year-old girl in shock. "What is this a joke"? Sarah looked right back at him and said "No, I want to have consensual sex, will you have sex with me"? Chip got up and walked out of McDonalds leaving Sarah sitting there.

Two weeks later, he saw her walking home from school and pulled over; "Get in," he said, "I will give you a ride home." She got in, and he said, "Ok, are you serious? Do you really want to do this? Why do you want to do this, and if we do it, no one can ever know – I am not going to go to jail for this."

They had sex that afternoon, afterwards Chip said, "You were not a virgin," and Sarah replied, "I never said I was; I said I wanted to have consensual sex with you."

It was a turning point in Sarah's life. She began to use sex as a way of getting men to do things for her. She and, her girlfriend Ginny, enjoyed going dancing but because they were, only 17 the girls often got turned away from the dance clubs. Sarah knew a few guys in their 30's who were always eager to take out young girls in the hopes of having an enjoyable evening later. For the most part, Sarah and Ginny would ditch these guys during the evening, laughing as they ran away. However, sometimes they were not so lucky, and the girls had to deliver on their promises.

Between alcohol and the promiscuity, Sarah began to lose herself. Going from one man to another she could not seem to find what she was craving, her heart still dissatisfied.

She came home one day to find Ruth on the couch, with a guy that was 19 year's old. His name was John, and he was the brother of one of Sarah's friends. Ruth looked at Sarah and said matter-of-factly, "John is moving in, I am pregnant with his baby."

"Oh good grief mother when are you going to grow up" yelled Sarah as she stormed out of the house. John did move in, and Sarah ignored them. It was her senior year of high school, and all she had to do was graduate so that she could find a job and move out.

That night was the beginning of a three-day drinking binge, which ended with her swallowing an entire bottle of aspirin. Her friend Judy stopped by the house and found her in the bedroom. Judy called her dad and he raced them to the hospital, where Sarah had her stomach pumped. Sarah spent one day in the ICU and two more days in the hospital. They released her with the stipulation that she had to go see a psychiatrist, "Yeah sure, whatever" said Sarah.

The following day Sarah had an appointment with a Dr. Ure, and they talked for a while. Dr. Ure interrupted Sarah and said, "I do not think your living conditions are safe. If I send you home, I think this is going to happen again." She looked Sarah dead in the eyes and asked, "If I send you home will you try to kill yourself again?"

"Yes" Sarah said without a moment of hesitation, she knew in her heart would try again, because inside Sarah was already dead.

The doctor made a few phone calls; first, she called social services, to find out if there were any foster homes available. She was saddened by the news that no homes were available in Watertown to take someone of Sarah's age.

Then she called the children's psychiatric unit in Ogdensburg. She explained to Sarah that she could go there for 72 hours and be released. As the doctor was making arrangements, a blizzard had, and the normal transports that were available between Watertown and Ogdensburg were shut down. However, Dr. Ure was determined to get Sarah to the hospital and drove to Sarah's house to pack some clothes, before dropping her off at Mercy hospital where a sheriff would pick her up.

The normal 1.5-hour drive took about 4 hours as the sheriff's car crawled up Route 37. The whole time Sarah was sitting in the back thinking what have I done? I should have lied to the doctor. I must be crazy like my mother; they are going to lock me up.

What Sarah did not realize is that this was the first step she took towards breaking free of the abuse that she had endured for so many years. Because most of the abuse occurred under Ruth's watch, Sarah was not released from the children's ward until her 18th birthday, which was in June. Even then, she was not released to her home, but instead released to a halfway house.

Sarah graduated from high school that June and worked for a year to save up money for college. Over the course of the year, she was treated by Dr. Ure who took it upon herself to give the girl a chance. Dr. Ure even opened her home to Sarah during the summer and college breaks.

For Sarah, the time in the hospital was a time for her to learn some things about herself. While there, she learned that, she did not deserve the abuse that she had endured for so many years. She learned that she could have healthy relationships that were not based upon sex alone and were not harmful. She also came to realize that though there were many adults that turned a blind eye to what was going on, that there were many more that wanted to help.

Dr. Ure became a very important person in Sarah's life for many years. A nurse from the hospital became a role model, and a math teacher at the hospital became a second mother to Sarah. Through the women who took time out of their own lives, Sarah learned that she did not have to be a victim anymore; that being a victim only allowed the abusers to continue to win the war.

Epilogue

Ruth died in 2004 from emphysema. Primarily due to Ruth's maturing and Sarah's ability to forgive and accept people for whom they are, Ruth and Sarah were able to develop a relationship that somewhat resembled one of mother and daughter. Though the two women would never become close, there was a shared love between them. They never talked about those years with Marie; it was if neither of them could handle the memories if they did.

One day the phone rang, and it was Sarah's stepfather explaining that she needed to come home immediately; Ruth may not make it through the night. He put the phone to Ruth's lips and the garbled words could be vaguely heard through the phone "I love you baby girl".

It was a long flight from San Diego to Albany that night, and the whole time the 39-year-old Sarah kept reliving her life like a bad dream. Arriving early the following morning, she was greeted by her two youngest brothers, her step-dad, and various relatives that had congregated for the final hours. Sarah went into her mother's bedroom and looked at the helpless woman lying on the bed in the coma.

Helping the hospice nurse, they bathed Ruth. Just as the bath was finished and Ruth was re-dressed, her final breath escaped from her lips. Tears streamed down Sarah's face as she kissed her mother goodbye one final time. Tears for the years of pain, tears for the loss of childhood, and tears for the loss of her mother. Despite her not being perfect, Ruth was Sarah's mother. Sarah realized in that moment, the love that was in her own heart towards her mother.

The facts within this book are true. Names have been changed to protect the lives of the innocent and yes to protect some of the guilty. This book was not written for retribution. This book was written to help others realize that there are more out there like you, which have walked this path. You are not alone. Do not stop reaching out to others for help, do not give up, and most importantly, do not lose hope.

Message from the Author

I lived my life in the shadows. I lived my life in shame. For years, I hid my secrets from everyone that I cared about, because I did not want them to consider me broken. I am not broken, I am a survivor. I have done what is necessary to break the chain of violence in my own life. I did what was necessary to make sure that I did not pass it down to my own children.

Children are suffering from a hidden epidemic of child abuse and neglect. Every year 3.3 million reports of child abuse are made in the United States, involving nearly 6 million children.

When I published my story initially, some of my closest friends were shocked and saddened. They had no idea what my life was like. That is how well child abuse is hidden.

Types of Child Abuse:

- Neglect – 78.3%
- Physical Abuse – 17.6%
- Sexual Abuse – 9.2%
- Psychological Maltreatment – 8.1%
- Medical Neglect – 2.4%
- Other – 10.3%

Note that these numbers add up to more than 100%, because it not uncommon for a child to suffer more than one type of abuse.

I myself suffered from physical, sexual, psychological abuse, and neglect. There were times in my teenage years, which I would have gone hungry, or slept in a house with no heat, if not for the families that let me stay at their homes.

Do you suspect a case of child abuse or are you being abused yourself? You can get help: 1-800-4-A-CHILD. The National Hotline is staffed 24/7 with qualified crisis counselors.

Child Abuse Statistics:

- A report of child abuse is made in the United States every 10 seconds.
- More than five children die each day as a result of child abuse.
- 80% of those children that die from child abuse are under the age of 4.
- 50-60% of child fatalities due to abuse are not even recognized and documented on death certificates.
- 90% or more of juvenile sexual abuse victims know their perpetrator.
- Child abuse has no socioeconomic barriers; it crosses all lines, and can be found in all religions and educational levels.
- Approximately 30% of abused and neglected children will continue the cycle of abuse by abusing their own children.
- It costs the United States an estimated $124 billion a year to help children of abuse and neglect.

Below is some information to help you identify if you are in an abusive relationship.

- What is domestic violence?

- Common Warning Signs of Domestic Violence (PDF)

- Understanding DV: The Power and Control Wheel (PDF)

- How to Help a Loved One: Do's and Do nots (PDF)

- The American Humane Association has information about how to report child sexual abuse.

Shadowfyre Publications

<u>I Love You Baby Girl</u> – Part I of the two part series: Not a Victim... But a Survivor. The true story of a young girl, which lived a life of torture and extreme child abuse.

<u>I Learned to Love Myself</u> – Part II of the two part series: Not a Victim... But a Survivor. The continuation of the true story of Sarah as she makes her way from childhood into young adulthood, leaving behind the mentality of a victim and becoming a survivor.

<u>Not a Victim… But a Survivor</u> – The entire series compiled into one book. Additional text included by the author.

About The Author

Born and raised in a quiet upstate New York town nestled between the St. Lawrence and Lake Ontario, Watertown, NY. In 1997, Desire, transplanted herself from the city that is sometimes known to be colder than Alaska, to San Diego, California! Though there are times when she experiences nostalgic moments about snow, those moments are fleeting, and she truly enjoys the "year round" warmth that she experiences in San Diego.

Desire has been writing for many years for small targeted audiences and has recently decided to start publishing some of her works to reach a broader audience. As a voracious reader for years, she appreciates many different types of books, from biographies to science fiction. Desire Night started off her career as a teacher and moved into developing educational software for classrooms in the late 90's.

You can find out more about what Desire is writing by visiting her website at http://www.desirenight.com.

Did this book touch you – let the author know at author@desirenight.com

References

Child Help (2013). Prevention and Treatment of Child Abuse. http://www.childhelp.org/

Fang, X., et al. The economic burden of child maltreatment in the United States and implications for prevention. Child Abuse & Neglect (2012), doi:10.1016/j.chiabu.2011.10.006 Retrieved from: http://www.sciencedirect.com/science/article/pii/S0145213411003140

Glen Kaiser; 1995 Parting Glance, Rez Band, Lament.

Harlow, C. U.S. Department of Justice, Office of Justice Programs. (1999).Prior abuse reported by inmates and probationers (NCJ 172879) Retrieved from

http://bjs.ojp.usdoj.gov/content/pub/pdf/pari
p.pdf

Long - Term Consequences of Child Abuse and
Neglect. Child Welfare Information
Gateway.Washington, D.C.: U.S.
Department of Health and Human Services,
2006. Retrieved from
http://www.childwelfare.gov/pubs/factsheets
/long_term_consequences.cfm

National Council on Child Abuse and Family
Violence. Parental Substance Abuse A Major
Factor In Child Abuse And Neglect.
Retrieved from
http://www.nccafv.org/parentalsubstanceabu
se.htm

Parental substance abuse. Retrieved from
http://www.childwelfare.gov/can/factors/par
entcaregiver/substance.cfm

Roger Hodgson; 1979 The Logical Song,
Supertramp's Breakfast in America album.

Snyder, Howard, N. (2000, July). Sexual assault
of young children as reported to law
enforcement: victim, incident, and offender
characteristics. Retrieved from
http://bjs.ojp.usdoj.gov/content/pub/pdf/sayc
rle.pdf

Swan, N. (1998). Exploring the role of child
abuse on later drug abuse: Researchers face
broad gaps in information. NIDA Notes,
13(2). Retrieved from the National Institute
on Drug Abuse website:
www.nida.nih.gov/NIDA_Notes/NNVol13N2
/exploring.html

U.S. Department of Health and Human Services
Administration for Children and Families
Administration on Children, Youth and
Families Children's Bureau.Child Abuse and
Neglect Fatalities 2009: Statistics and

Interventions. Retrieved from
http://www.childwelfare.gov/pubs/factsheets/fatality.pdf

U.S. Department of Health and Human Services, Administration for Children and Families, Administration on Children, Youth and Families, Children's Bureau. (2011). Child Maltreatment 2010. Available from http://www.acf.hhs.gov/programs/cb/stats_research/index.htm#can

United States Government Accountability Office, 2011. Child maltreatment: strengthening national data on child fatalities could aid in prevention (GAO-11-599). Retrieved from http://www.gao.gov/new.items/d11599.pdf

Printed in Great Britain
by Amazon